HOME

The editorial staff of *Miracle Monocle* is pleased to reveal the third volume in its micro-anthology series. This ongoing, innovative publishing initiative will employ digital publishing techniques to address underserved communities in the literary world. Our hope is to offer worthy voices a new platform for expression and to illuminate underexplored territories for our readers.

HOME

A *Miracle Monocle* Micro-Anthology

Miracle Monocle
Louisville, Kentucky

First Printing: 2022

ISBN-13: 978-1-7341233-2-6

Miracle Monocle
University of Louisville
Bingham Humanities 315
2216 S. 1st Street
Louisville, KY 40292
louisville.edu/miraclemonocle

Ordering Information: Copies of this book are available via the *Miracle Monocle* website and other online vendors. Special discounts are available on quantity purchases by corporations, associations, educators, and others. For details, please contact the publisher at the above listed address.

U.S. trade bookstores and wholesalers: Please contact *Miracle Monocle* at the above listed address.

HOME

A *Miracle Monocle* Micro-Anthology

Miracle Monocle
Louisville, Kentucky

First Printing: 2022

ISBN-13: 978-1-7341233-2-6

Miracle Monocle
University of Louisville
Bingham Humanities 315
2216 S. 1st Street
Louisville, KY 40292
louisville.edu/miraclemonocle

Ordering Information: Copies of this book are available via the *Miracle Monocle* website and other online vendors. Special discounts are available on quantity purchases by corporations, associations, educators, and others. For details, please contact the publisher at the above listed address.

U.S. trade bookstores and wholesalers: Please contact *Miracle Monocle* at the above listed address.

EDITOR'S NOTE

This book was conceived and executed by the editorial staff of *Miracle Monocle*, an award-winning literary journal housed at the University of Louisville. Our efforts were made possible by the generous support of the University of Louisville, the College of Arts and Sciences, the Department of English, the Program in Creative Writing, and donors like you.

We'd like to thank all of the writers who shared their words with us; the response to our call for entries was marvelous and encouraging. We hope you keep creating homes wherever life finds you.

This book would not have been possible without the hard work and creative energies of our student editors, who are celebrated on our masthead. We welcome readers to share their thoughts about this book on our website: louisville.edu/miraclemonocle

Warmly,

Dr. Sarah Anne Strickley
Faculty Editor of *Miracle Monocle*

Miracle Monocle

Miracle Monocle is an online journal of innovative literary and visual art. Published bi-annually, the journal features poems, short stories, literary nonfiction, and a broad range of experimental works. The journal is staffed by a team of graduate and undergraduate editors who earn course credit for assisting in the production of our issues. A faculty editor guides the editorial process and creative writing faculty consult on the growth of the journal. Previously unpublished and emerging writers are highly encouraged to submit. Please visit our archives to sample issues of the journal and read our submission guidelines. Information about supporting *Miracle Monocle* is also available online; all donations are tax deductible to the extent allowed by the law.

Visit us online here:
Website: www.louisville.edu/miraclemonocle
Twitter: @miracle_monocle
Facebook: @miraclemonocle
Instagram: @miraclemonocle

TABLE OF CONTENTS

THE DEER BONE 1
Aza Pace

UNDER THE DOGWOOD 2
Christine Beck

COMPENSATION 5
Matthew E. Henry

FEVER DREAM 6
Skye Jackson

WHAT IS MORE GENEROUS THAN A WINDOW? 8
Gloria Heffernan

WHAT'S NEW IN THE NEIGHBORHOOD 10
Devon Balwit

ON HISTORIES WE WILL NEVER KNOW 11
David Olimpio

NOTES ON *E.T.*, NOW THAT WE ARE BOTH IN OUR FORTIES 17
Erin Keane

Contributors' Notes

THE DEER BONE

Aza Pace

A deer must die of old age sometimes.
There is not always a hunter

who discovers he has shot
a doe out of season and leaves her

in the woods hoping no one will discover.
Sometimes, surely, an old deer must

lie down in a mossy place beneath a maple
and fall into the green All.

And then, if after a long time, my dog
returns home ebullient

with a still-furred deer bone in her jaws,
that does not mean anything

terrible has happened. After all, look how
content my dog is now

to spend all day in the front yard gnawing
the elbow joint to the marrow,

to be a part of the everything the deer
must have entered.

UNDER THE DOGWOOD

Christine Beck

The approach is familiar—a lane bordered by neat white fences along pastures that used to hold my grandfather's race horses—three retirees he said he'd care for until they died. The farm was sold ten years ago when my grandmother died. Today, I need to see it, show it to my little daughters, even though for them, it holds no memories, hoping they will intuit my connection with this bit of earth.

The house presents the same fieldstone face, square and upright, the stones varied in color with ivy climbing around the doorframe. The farm was named Ivy Rock. Two windows are centered on the first floor. Two identical windows peer out above. I can't tell if the curtains are the crisp organdy of my grandmother's day, a filmy flutter of misty fabric. Are they washed and starched each Monday as when I was a child? Is there a glass candy dish of M&M's, a dish that no matter how carefully I lifted it, would always transmit a telltale signal to my grandmother that I was sneaking a treat? Does one dining chair seat still hold a huge Audubon bird book to boost a granddaughter to table level? And the magazines—does the new owner read *Woman's Day*, *Good Housekeeping*, the *Reader's Digest*, tucked neatly in a magazine rack beside the leather armchair? Does a "grandmother clock," half the size of the typical floor-to-ceiling grandfather variety, pose primly on the mantel with its inscrutable sun and moon icons where numbers should be, chiming out the hours of a well-regulated life?

As we park in the space beneath the huge bell, the one I was always implored not to ring lest it rouse the neighbors to an emergency, I see the new owners have put an addition on the back of the house. I've already rehearsed my speech. There was no way to call ahead as I didn't know who lived there. I knocked. A woman opened the door. "Hi, this used to be my grandparents' farm. We're visiting from Connecticut. Would you mind if I show my daughters around?"

"Of course, come in. Feel free to look around."

After I admire the addition, we visit the barn. Today, it has no horses. Instead, a few chickens skitter and cluck around my daughters' knees, scaring them, suburban children used only to gerbils and guinea pigs, predictable and caged. I then usher my girls where I've intended all along—the dogwood tree in the front meadow. I planted it thirteen years ago after placing a square metal box in the hole I'd dug. The box, about eight by ten inches, with an engraved faceplate, held my mother's ashes, dead at the age of fifty from breast cancer. I don't remember who was there with me—my grandmother for sure, perhaps my brothers.

But there were no prayers, no music, no remembrances. Just a shovel, dirt, and a small dogwood tree. This was what she wanted, her ashes to be buried under any tree at Ivy Rock. There had already been a service, a gathering of friends and relatives. We were out of words, numb and bereft beneath the afternoon sun shining on my grandmother's rose garden nearby, standing in the space of a yawning future in an expanse of newly mown grass.

My daughters are too young. I know that. They don't know death, can't imagine their mother won't always be around serving chicken nuggets, making costumes for Japan Day at school, or cheering at a soccer game. I hope they never find a note in my handwriting on yellow-lined legal paper that's labelled "Funeral Instructions," specifying the flowers or music I'd like for my memorial.

As if we'd planned a picnic, I pose my little girls around the tree, like spring buds yet to unfold on a dogwood in April. Eleanor, my eldest, wears a red jumper, captured in the photo I tuck in an album. The girls' blonde hair shimmers in the sun. They smile. Smile for mama.

I know we'll never visit here again. I've used my one excuse to the stranger who lives where we once gathered for family dinners, swung from the huge old oak, gathered watercress down by the brook. I silently offer these children to the grandmother who never got to see them.

"Here," I say, "here is what I've done to honor you. These little girls, bright as the red geraniums you asked for, these are my memorial."

COMPENSATION

Matthew E. Henry

midrash qatan on Genesis 4:25-32

most mornings she thinks of Havah—Mother Eve—
who understood the constricted chest
of squandering forever with the wrong tree,
with the wrong man. of waking one morning to find
yourself seen as only a wedding present and
there's no gift receipt for love. she hates herself

for calling Havah blessed because 2/3 of her children
were buried beyond Eden's embrace. her own are down
the hall, eyes closed and abed. another growing
in her closest silence. she readies their breakfast, packs
their lunches. but first, puts on the coffee. he'll be up soon.
she marvels that her bones once cleaved to his.

her flesh once spoke in angelic tongues at his touch.
but that's all gone the way of dust and ashes.
conversations with church friends turn her mind
to *Job*—how people fear seeing their sadness
reflected in another's eyes, will believe the lies
they wish were true. she thinks of his nameless wife

and her bravery. most nights she dreams of Mother Hagar.
of fleeing into the wilderness—her children under her ribs,
safe in their car seats, like arrows strapped to her back.
of driving somewhere south, somewhere warm. of keeping
her eyes fixed ahead—pedal down—until she sees a sign
for a cheap, clean motel with an ocean view

in a good school district.

FEVER DREAM

Skye Jackson

my mama stepped
from fever into dream
one night

she wished for my great-grandmother
and suddenly she was standing
in front of her house

said it was exactly
as she remembered it
before katrina
with the pale silver gate too

and when she walked in
she saw the mantelpiece
as it stood before the panels
were warped by moisture
and covered
with black mold

she passed
pictures of herself
pigtailed and peter pan collared
frozen in seventies sepia tint
and focused her gaze
on the open doorway
to the kitchen

her long dead grandmother
ophelia,
or as her children called her,

Mother,
stood at the stove
and stirred a pot of red beans
when my mama heard her say
sit down, child, & rest some

my mama buried her face
in her small light hands

& the minutes
dripped by
on the old wooden clock
in the hall

she sat in her dead grandmother's
dead kitchen & cried
until she woke up
alone, pillows damp

later, she called me
& said:

skye why didn't i ask her
what i needed to?

how come all i could do
in her presence
was cry?

i just listened
to my mama
because i knew
that's what she needed
instead of the sweet
emptiness
of a daughter's
naïve reply

WHAT IS MORE GENEROUS THAN A WINDOW?

Gloria Heffernan

(A Cento Comprised of Lines from *Poetry of Presence: An Anthology of Mindfulness Poems*)

1. Stop whatever it is you're doing.
2. Come, let's stand by the window.
3. I have seen the sun break through.
4. Together, we are a tribe of eyes that look upward.
5. The evening arrives; we look up and it is there.
6. Invisible birds sing to the memory of light.
7. The trees stand like twenty-seven prophets in a field.
8. Whatever it is, the trees know
9. every thought and action is sacred.
10. Wherever you are is called Here.
11. What fools we were, not to have seen
12. from the place we are right now.
13. The world is still beautiful.
14. Go and open the door.

Gloss:

Title: "The Patience of Ordinary Things," Pat Schneider
1. "On How to Pick and Eat Poems," Phyllis Cole Dai
2. "Thinking," Danusha Lameris
3. "The Bright Field," R.S. Thomas
4. "We are a Tribe," Alberto Rios
5. "Surprised by Evening," Robert Bly
6. "Still Life at Dusk," Rosemerry Wahtola Trommer
7. "I am Going to Start Living Like a Mystic," Edward Hirsch
8. "Learning from Trees," Grace Butcher
9. "Now is the Time," Hafiz (translation by Daniel Ladinsky)
10. "Lost," David Wagoner

11. “Meeting the Light Completely,” Jane Hirschfield
12. “The Place Where We are Right,” Yehuda Amichai (translation by Chana Bloch and Stephen Mitchell)
13. “Testimony,” Rebecca Baggett
14. “the door,” Miraslov Holub (translation by Ian and Jarmila Milner et al.)

WHAT'S NEW IN THE NEIGHBORHOOD

Devon Balwit

All around, the buyers are renovating,
additions towering over the concrete statuettes
of the Holy Mother on the lawns of the Catholic
retirees. I can almost hear the prices rising
by tens of thousands each year. I snag a flier
from a realtor's box, square footage and upgrades,
though I know it's out of the reach of my children.
My death alone will pass them keys
to the patch jobs that have worked well enough
to warm their father and me after our daily constitutionals.
I'm almost eager to be reduced
to bare foundation, for another to do
what I could never manage myself.

ON HISTORIES WE WILL NEVER KNOW

David Olimpio

1.

I was conceived in a house on a street called Overwood Drive. All the streets in that section of Olney, Maryland were named Something-wood. Overwood, Archwood, Prestwood. Our house was only three houses away from the intersection of Overwood and Morningwood.

If only I had been conceived on Morningwood. (I mean, I suppose maybe I was.) But as far as the street name, it was definitely Overwood, unfortunately. We, each of us, in our minds, make tiny legends of ourselves, our childhoods, our lives. A conception on Morningwood Drive would have fit nicely into mine.

But thanks to somebody's arbitrary demarcation of streets and houses, I can not write that particular mythology of myself, even though the incident in question probably happened only a couple hundred feet from a home with an address that would have made such a statement factually accurate.

Then again, maybe the naming of those streets isn't arbitrary at all, but integral to the entire shebang of my being here, to the Shebang of David, as it were. If my parents had wound up living in a house on Morningwood Drive, maybe I wouldn't have been conceived at all. Or maybe a soul would have been brought into existence, but it wouldn't have been my soul exactly, even if the body still looked like mine.

Maybe that Morningwood soul was indeed brought into existence but on a different timeline than the one in which I am writing this, the one in which you are now reading it. Maybe Morningwood Drive me isn't a writer at all. Maybe he is a world famous conceptual physicist and Olympic Swimmer. Maybe Morningwood Drive me is the one who, on that timeline, won gold at the 2000 Summer Olympics in Sydney in the 50 meter freestyle, instead of Gary Hall, Jr.

I'm sure I will find out the answer to all of this if I watch a dozen more YouTube videos on time and relativity.

2.

The house on Overwood Drive was technically my first home, though the entire time I spent inside of it, I also spent inside the body of my mother. My parents moved to a different house by the time I came physically into the world. And so really it was more my mother that was my home while on Overwood, not the house.

But isn't that always kind of the case? Our homes aren't so much about the places as they are the people we're in those places with. My parents divorced when I was six, and I lived primarily with my mom in one house for most of my childhood. After I moved out on my own, my mom lived in two other homes, and even though those places were never my primary residences, they still felt like "home" to me because she was in them.

It had taken quite a bit of effort on the part of my parents to make the Shebang of Me happen. Today, they might have been encouraged to try IVF, but in the early 1970s, that was still more science-fiction to many people than science. What my parents were offered by the medical community was anecdotal advice. According to my dad, this mostly consisted of trying various positions.

Until 2015, which was about four years after my mom passed away, I thought I knew the basic facts of my mother's life as far as children were concerned. The mother I knew the entire time she was alive was a mother who had one son in November of 1973 and, before that, a daughter (my half-sister) a little over a decade earlier during a previous marriage.

I also knew that my mom had twins during that previous marriage, conceived shortly after my sister was born. One was stillborn and the other died shortly after coming into the world. I did some research through a newspaper archive a few years ago and found an obituary for the one who had been born alive. She lived 9 days. She had been named Katherine, which is also, coincidentally, the name of my ex-wife (though she spelled her name with a C).

What I hadn't known was there had been another child, born before my sister, and placed for adoption. This all happened away from my mother's family and her home and in a different state many miles away. She never told anybody about it. I learned about it after this first son of hers found and contacted me in 2015 as I was just finishing my first collection of essays which included several pieces about my mom. He wrote me a short email explaining who he was, and nothing has been the same since then.

He and I got to know one another. He recently passed away due to complications of ALS, and I feel fortunate I was able to meet him and spend some time with him while he was still alive. His home, for the last decade or so of his life, was a single room inside an assisted-living facility. All he wanted was to be known. To be seen for who he was. His name was Ken, and he was my mom's first-born son. He had two daughters. One of them looks remarkably like my mom.

There is much more to this story. But the part that feels necessary for the purposes of this story here is the idea of how my mom always felt like "home" to me. And how she still feels like home, even though there was something I never knew about her which completely changed the mythology of her I'd made in my mind.

Finding all of this out has been hugely disorienting for me. There has been a lot of confusion and disbelief and denial. Sometimes I've felt happy and grateful. Other times, I've been angry, for reasons I can't fully explain. But mostly what I've felt is a deep empathy and love for my mom, and a strange sense of loss for a history I will never fully know.

I know she must have felt ashamed and embarrassed about this aspect of her past. She maybe felt a lot of guilt. Maybe all of this is why she did not want me or other people close to her to know. Maybe she thought it would make me feel more distant from her. But for me it has had the opposite effect. I feel like I understand my mom better now, and it's made me feel even closer to her. I think her close friends and family all would have felt the same way if they had known, and it makes me sad that she had to carry that by herself.

I never understood during my mother's lifetime the full extent of what it probably meant to her to have me, to be in that house on Overwood Drive carrying me, unashamed and unencumbered, but perhaps unconsciously shadowed by those past traumas. I wonder if she was scared. But I also wonder if she felt like she was home for the first time. It's one of the things I'd like to ask her if I could.

3.

As an adult, I have lived in two houses of my own which also happened to be named after a kind of wood: Beech and Hickory. And similar to my parents, while my then-wife and I lived in these homes, we were intermittently engaged in the activity of trying to make a baby. Because it was no longer science fiction in 2014, some of those attempts involved IVF. Also, we did a lot of tracking of time and cycles. We didn't worry so much about positions, though.

None of these attempts were successful, save for one. And, as it turns out, this one successful attempt wasn't even so much an "attempt," which is to say, we had no longer been "trying." Instead, we had decided we would adopt and were on a list at an open adoption agency.

I remember standing in the house on Hickory, in the hallway outside our newly renovated guest bathroom, and seeing the result on that stick. It seemed improbable if not completely impossible: that after many deliberate, though ultimately unsuccessful attempts, we had managed to become pregnant quite by accident. That day was Mother's Day 2014. It had been a little over three years since my mom had died.

Up to that point, I don't think the house on Hickory had felt completely like a home to either my wife or me. We'd been in the house for five years, but our living room and dining room still felt "under construction." We'd done some work in our bedroom, ripping up the carpet and painting the walls, but we weren't really happy with the color. The house was quite beautiful and homey, but the walls lacked proper insulation which made it drafty in winter. My favorite room was the backyard. These are all literal facts, but they make wonderful metaphors, I guess. I love when nonfiction works out that way.

The house never felt more like a home than the day we read the results on that stick and cried together in the hallway. And it never felt less like a home than the numbing, lost days and months and years we continued to exist in that house after we had to terminate the pregnancy at 15 weeks.

During the time we were going to be parents, I remember feeling so much purpose and hope. I had started working on painting her nursery. After the termination, I finished the painting but we no longer knew what to do with the room. It sat empty for over a year. Most of the time, the door was closed.

We were no longer at home in that house. But worse, we were no longer at home in one another.

4.

For the planners of the neighborhood where I was conceived, naming the streets with the surname "wood" required no small amount of imagination and optimism. I mention this because there is a photo of the house from that time and, in it, everything had that look of just being freshly built, and there was very little in the way of wood to be seen for miles. The small one-story house appears even smaller against the backdrop of flat land and big sky. The only vertical structures visible were the tall transmission towers looming in the distance, delivering power to this newly suburbanized area of what had probably once been farmland.

My sister went back to the house during a high school reunion and took a photo from the then-present of 2017. The house, the entire neighborhood, had arrived unto itself, the streets had come into their names. The yards were now populated by tall trees. The grass, which had been spare and still showing dirt in 1970, was now thick and green. You could no longer see the transmission towers behind what had at one time been our home.

Everything in the 2017 photo looks so firmly rooted, like the house, the trees, the car in the driveway are all exactly where they are supposed to be.

If you didn't know about the earlier photo, it would be hard to imagine it any other way.

NOTES ON *E.T.*, NOW THAT WE ARE BOTH IN OUR FORTIES

Erin Keane

Let's begin with the pre-history: the horror film that never was, John Sayles' script for *Night Skies*, Steven Spielberg's first idea for a sort of spiritual sequel to *Close Encounters of the Third Kind*, intended as a fright feature based loosely on the real-life 1955 Kelly. UFO encounter in rural Western Kentucky, with its infamous little green men waging war on local farmers. Except maybe in reality, they were just territorial owls dodging shotgun blasts, the supposed invading spaceships nothing more, or less, miraculous than a meteor shower. Who's to say? One person's terror is another's farce.

The Kelly Encounter did get its movie, kind of, a few years after Sayles' *Night Skies* script was scrapped (to be reimagined as the standalone story *E.T. the Extraterrestrial*, which premiered on June 11, 1982). The 1986 horror-comedy *Critters* borrowed some of its premise from the Kelly Encounter and became a cult classic, spawning four sequels and a TV series reboot.

In real life, the actual Kentucky community of Kelly now celebrates its notorious encounter every year with Little Green Men Days, a family-friendly festival featuring flying saucer-shaped bounce houses and enough green face paint to cover a barn: revision as reclamation, the likeliest war to break out started by a full funnel cake stomach invading the Gravitron's spin.

* * *

There is no *E.T.* cinematic multiverse to keep track of. Spielberg considers it "a closed story," which means no tortured sequels, no painful animated spin-off where the kids and the alien botanist, I don't know, solve mysteries and thwart the hapless feds, no reboot starring a smart-alecky kid with cool hair. We don't always know how to leave a good thing alone. But when the alien botanist tells Elliott, "Be good," what he means is, *you are*. End of story.

In this homage economy, a lack of sequels doesn't necessarily mean a story can be at rest. For instance, *E.T.'s* bony fingerprints, including his iconic bicycle flight, are all over Netflix's horror-nostalgia series *Stranger Things*. The currency chain of allegiance passes through so many hands: From Michael speaking in Yoda's voice and Elliott walking E.T. through the *Star Wars* cast of action figures to Eleven hiding out in Mike's house, wandering Hawkins, Indiana, in a wig and dress. Each of these bits carries the texture of its antecedents; together they operate under a grand unified theory of *if you know, you know*.

"Once we were young, and films were beautiful," wrote *TIME* film critic Richard Corliss on the occasion of the twentieth anniversary of *E.T.*, a feeling which is impossible to recapture as adults, and yet still we try, recycling motifs and borrowing images and collaging them into a map that will lead us back to that feeling. The industry has long rewarded this fidelity—sequel pressure predates *E.T.*—but the intensity of the dedication to franchise has started to feel like a never-ending school reunion: Class of 1990-Whatever, together forever, in hologram form even after death.

"We could grow up together," Elliott pleaded, trying to convince E.T to stay with him instead of flying back to his home planet. But E.T. was already grown. Was he born knowing how to heal? Unlikely. Probably he studied, and apprenticed, and made a lot of mistakes, took what he learned and made it his own. Magic is just our word for the moment when sustained attention finally, suddenly, snaps into its intended shape. Maybe there's no real harm in focusing much of that attention on small revisions to what has already been done, in trading discovery for comfort. But love demands we leave ourselves room to grow apart, a lesson we forget over and over, no matter Elliott's promise, Eleven's incandescent rage. We would rather revel in a curse: May you live long enough to see all your formative memories revised first into references, then into kitsch.

* * *

Which is how I should feel about the *E.T.* Adventure dark ride at Universal Studios, but I confess I don't. Riding it is a ritual that feels like stepping back in time, which is at least half the point of visiting a theme park as an adult. On my personal map of holy sites, it ranks somewhere between the Ryman Auditorium and the actual Muir Woods. This ride is more than thirty years old, does not require 3-D glasses, and features a lot of Day-Glo and a John Williams score. If they ever try to tear it down for a *Despicable Me* expansion, I will do my best to start a BMX riot.

You enter and stand in line on a path ringed with fabricated redwoods and illuminated in alien green, then mount up on janky bikes designed to look like the ones we rode as children, a crate strapped to the front with a shrouded little body tucked inside. Attached to a track, we glide past NASA scientists in space suits and federal agents, up, up, over the tops of the cop cars, their red and blue lights spinning, into the trees, and then breaking out of the forest, the town twinkling in miniature below, further, further, past the Amblin moon and through a blanket of stars, then into a hyperspace jump, and now we're on the botanist's Green Planet, little dudes like him everywhere, and it's lush and damp and ringed with gigantic psychedelic blooms.

Manufactured as it is, the simplicity of the story, with its beginning, middle, and end—a bike, a flight, the discovery of another world—is soothing and best savored on repeat, like re-watching a favorite movie. Exit through the gift shop to replay the ritual. To get back to where I am trying to go, I have to wait, walk, ride, turn around, go again.

* * *

Although Spielberg decided against making a horror movie, enlisting the magical Melissa Mathison to write a screenplay about a friendship between a lonely boy and an abandoned alien that became *E.T. the Extra-Terrestrial* instead, he still made a story built on pain. Spielberg says the movie was informed by his parents' divorce; for my money, also it's the best movie I've seen about a child losing a parent and no adults taking your grief seriously even though it disrupts every known rule of your universe. How the pain sneaks into your house and takes up residence in your closet without ever being acknowledged. How it can touch all your stuff, feed on little bits of you freely given because you can see yourself as well as some unknowable darkness in its wide, hungry eyes. How it comforts you when nothing else can.

Elliott is a child in mourning, which nobody around him wants to talk about or help him through. His father has disappeared, and he's expected to carry on, not be selfish, not make it about what he has lost. Kids were supposed to be resilient. "He's in Mexico with Sally," but his father might as well be on the moon, might as well have landed on some distant planet in another solar system, not going to be home for dinner tonight or any other, working late for lightyears to come.

A parent, or an idea of a family, becomes extra-terrestrial like that—severed from the world, scattered into distant points you'll spend the rest of your life connecting, dot by dot, into a constellation outline of a whole body, no distress signal powerful enough to reach.

* * *

When Elliott shows the alien botanist where he is on the globe, it's clearly Southern California. In the southwestern suburban desert I knew, with similar colors and textures woven through the landscape around the set of their family home, there was no Endor, no towering redwoods a bike ride away. Here, also, a dreamscape cornfield touching the edge of the nighttime yard. What scrubby desert cul-de-sac had such green for its borders? But the dissonance didn't confuse me. Hadn't I once woken up in a city facing skyscrapers and gone to bed in the shadow of the Gila Mountains? If the botanist could travel here from another planet, why couldn't Elliott bike from the outskirts of Los Angeles to almost Oregon in a few minutes?

"Elliott thinks its thoughts?" the clueless adult asks.

"No. Elliott feels his feelings," his brother answers.

There's a video called *Everything Wrong with E.T. the Extra-Terrestrial*, made by the people who make those videos that count a movie's sins, which is to say, story quirks we once accepted on faith. It has more than 1.3 million plays and counting. It's fast and entertaining, but it's also a model for how we can lose the distinction between criticizing and criticism, between the first and second definitions, walking into one and coming out the other.

Dissection isn't always the best way to understand a body. To love is also to suspend disbelief in death for long enough to form a bond. "Be good," the botanist says by way of saying goodbye. Loss, and what follows, can make tinkering monsters out of us all.

* * *

When *E.T.* turned twenty, Spielberg made some adjustments. Gone were the FBI agent guns, replaced digitally by walkie-talkies. As if guns were the horror in the film and not the image of astronauts cresting the subdivision hill, their slow march to Elliott's house backlit by the setting sun. The men in the moon suits, our heroes, invading with ill intent, the wonder we projected onto them inverted against us.

Among the many things about *E.T.* that feel too real to be included in a mainstream kid's movie now because they were: insults like "penis-breath," the invocation of a lurking pervert, haphazard home furnishings, casual classroom brutality toward animals, unintentional emotional neglect, the parentification of Michael. And there is no trusted mentor adult in *E.T.*, just kids experiencing their world as it was and as it could be and learning fast how the authorities would fight to preserve the power of the status quo. You could put pool noodles in the cops' hands, and it wouldn't change a thing about that.

Ten years later, Spielberg restored the guns with a mea culpa, saying he realized "I had robbed people who loved *E.T.* of their memories of *E.T.*" The revision was a betrayal of a kind, however well-intentioned. But it's not that we loved or even needed the guns themselves. It's just a different kind of horror to be told by the man in charge that we didn't see what we knew we saw.

* * *

There is nothing left to say about the transfiguration of M&Ms in the script to Reese's Pieces. (M&Ms have controversial individual personalities now, as we all regret to know, but Everything Wrong with Literally Everything is not-great SEO.) Let us instead talk about Coors, about *E.T.* downing a can right out of the refrigerator and sending his buzz straight to Elliott in school.

As a kid I had a tiny figurine of E.T. frozen in that moment, which in the 1980s must have seemed okay but might not be found in the toy aisle today. The botanist's pose: can in hand, head turned to see where that racket was coming from, wearing that blue flannel shirt. A father conjured slant, made small enough to fit in a kid's hand.

I lost that toy like I lost my own father, just a couple of months before *E.T.* premiered: here one day, gone the next. I replace him, I lose him again. But there is eBay. This is what the internet excels at—never forcing us to move on. Over the course of my bidding, I have picked up other figurines, too, when packaged as a set: E.T. wrapped in the blanket, toting a Speak & Spell; E.T. in the wig and dress disguise; E.T. holding the blooming flowers. I tuck them inside the pots of my own plants which are always in need of something I can't figure out how to give: more or less light, drier or damper soil, the right food.

The tropical maranta leuconeura—the prayer plant, we call it—is native to Brazil, but I make myself believe it can thrive in my home office, that I can give it what it needs to grow. When water lifts its leaves from their drooping torpor, the minor act of resurrection makes me feel like I have powers. When I try to picture a prayer plant growing in the wild ground, my mind instead puts me back on the Universal Studios *E.T.* Adventure ride, gliding past an oversized plastic version, neon green with pink slashes, growing out of the fabricated rock, always thriving, always the same each time I pass it on the bike track.

* * *

When I watch *E.T.* now, in my forties, I think about that six-pack of beer and how Elliott's mother probably looked forward to cracking one open after a long day in a ruffled blouse navigating her stupid sexist office politics, the kids' bickering following them to bed. I can finally see how tired and scared and beautiful and young she is, how madly she is scrambling to hold her family together as it frays.

A family is never a closed story; there's always a revision waiting for the original script. "He hates Mexico!" she cries, a shitty memory of her shitty ex stuck playing on a loop in her head while he lives out his sequel with Sally. How she snaps when Elliott cries, "Dad would understand!" I get it now. I have been Elliott, nursing my hurt. I am relieved that I can watch the movie now and not feel his pain in the same way.

A slight fudge on the question of a sequel: In 2019, there was an extended cable-internet ad showing E.T. returning to Earth to visit Elliott, played once again by Henry Thomas, for the holidays. There is snow on the ground where Elliott lives, in a polished, ordered suburban home with a wife and two sweet, cheerful kids, to whom E.T. first reveals himself. Toys still befuddle the alien botanist; candy delights. It's fine for a commercial. All the fun beats remain—blink and you'll miss that Elliott still plays D&D—but the fear has been carefully excised, even though there's an ominous thing called the internet now, which the short movie slash long commercial is trying to sell by reminding us of when we were young and movies were beautiful, as if we are ever allowed to forget.

This is only a commercial, and maybe I should be offended by its egregious pandering to my cohort's nostalgia. But do you know what is missing in Elliott's serene adult cable internet-promoting home? There are no *Star Wars* action figures E.T.

once touched in display cases, no vintage Speak & Spell mounted on the wall, no conspiracy-map of reported UFO encounters since 1982. This is a choice, to go against the mood of the moment to deliver on the promise of Spielberg's original hopeful ending. Elliott has not become a bitter, broken crank, critically wounded by his brief encounter with magic abandoning him before he was ready, casting about for meaning, on a mission to deaden or redeem his pain. He has not, as far as we can tell, repeated the mistakes of his father, or spent the last several years pining for a time before he left. He just grew up; he found his own ways to heal. Maybe it's still a fantasy, this one designed to sell us comfort in middle-age. But it is also an adulthood Elliott deserves.

This essay originally appeared in Salon. *Reprinted with permission.*

CONTRIBUTORS' NOTES

AZA PACE's poems appear in *The Southern Review*, *Copper Nickel*, *Tupelo Quarterly*, *New Ohio Review*, *Passages North*, *Mudlark*, *Bayou Magazine*, and elsewhere. She's the winner of two Academy of American Poets University Prizes and an Inprint Donald Barthelme Prize in Poetry. She holds an MFA in Poetry from the University of Houston and is currently pursuing her PhD at the University of North Texas.

CHRISTINE BECK is a writer and teacher of literature and creative writing. She holds a MFA in Creative Writing and is a former Poet Laureate of West Hartford, CT. Her books of poetry include *Blinding Light* (Grayson Press, 2013), *I'm Dating Myself* (Dancing Girl Press, 2015), *Stirred, Not Shaken* (Five Oaks Press 2016) and *Beneath the Steps: a Writing Guide for 12-Step Recovery* (2019). She leads monthly workshops for writers in 12-step recovery. Her website is www.ChristineBeck.net.

MATTHEW E. HENRY is the author of *the Colored page* (Sundress Publications, 2022), *Teaching While Black* (Main Street Rag, 2020), and *Dust & Ashes* (Californios Press, 2020). He's an educator who earned his MFA in Creative Writing, MA in Theology, and PhD in Education. His poetry and prose has appeared in *Barren Magazine*, *Fahmidan Journal*, *The Florida Review*, *Identity Theory*, *Massachusetts Review*, *Ploughshares*, *Poetry East*, *Shenandoah*, and *Zone 3*. His website is www.MEHPoeting.com.

SKYE JACKSON was born and raised in New Orleans, Louisiana. She has served as a poetry editor for *Bayou Magazine* and several other publications. Her work has appeared or is forthcoming in *Electric Literature, Green Mountains Review*, *RATTLE,* and elsewhere. Her debut chapbook, *A Faster Grave*, won the 2019 Antenna Prize. She was also a finalist for the 2020 *RATTLE* Poetry Prize. In 2021, she won the AWP Intro Journals Award and was twice nominated for *Best New Poets*. Her work was recently selected by former U.S. Poet Laureate Billy Collins for inclusion in the Library of Congress Poetry 180 Program. This past spring, she was also crowned the winner of the legendary KGB Open Mic Contest in New York City. She served as the 2022 Writer-In-Residence at the Key West Literary Seminar in Florida and is currently attending the Regional Cave Canem Workshop in NYC.

GLORIA HEFFERNAN is the author of the poetry collection, *What the Gratitude List Said to the Bucket List* (New York Quarterly Books, 2019), and *Exploring Poetry of Presence: A Companion Guide for Readers, Writers and Workshop Facilitators* (Back Porch Productions, 2021) which won the 2021 Central New York Book Award for Non-fiction. She has written two chapbooks: *Hail to the Symptom* (Moonstone Press, 2019) and *Some of Our Parts* (Finishing Line Press, 2018). Her work has appeared in more than 100 publications, including *The Columbia Review*, *Stone Canoe*, and *The Perch*. Her website is www.gloriaheffernan.wordpress.com.

DEVON BALWIT's most recent collections are *Rubbing Shoulders with the Greats* (Seven Kitchens Press, 2020) and *Dog-Walking in the Shadow of Pyongyang* (Nixes Mate Books, 2021). Her website is www.pelapdx.wixsite.com/devonbalwitpoet.

DAVID OLIMPIO is the author of *This Is Not A Confession* (Awst Press, 2016) and has work in *The Missouri Review's Aud-Cast*, *jmww*, *Barrelhouse*, *Rappahannock Review*, *Crate*, and others. His website is www.davidolimpio.com.

ERIN KEANE is the author of *RUNAWAY: Notes on the Myths that Made Me* (Belt Publishing, 2022) and three collections of poems, and editor of *The Louisville Anthology*. She lives in Louisville, teaches in the Naslund-Mann Graduate School of Writing at Spalding University, and is editor-in-chief at *Salon*.

Miracle Monocle thanks you for the purchase of this book. We hope that you enjoyed it and will support future titles released in conjunction with our new publishing initiative: *The Miracle Monocle Micro-Anthology Series*. All proceeds from the sale of this book will go toward the realization of future titles in this series. Founded in 2009 as an annual digital literary journal, Miracle Monocle is now an AWP-award-winning biannual journal, as well as a training program for students with ambitions in the field of publishing, and a nexus of literary programming in Louisville, Kentucky. We pride ourselves on serving as a home for innovative literary art that might otherwise go unnoticed in a crowded media landscape; we are also committed to showcasing writers who might regularly escape the attention of traditional or commercial publishers. We take pleasure in juxtaposing emerging talent with established voices. For readers interested in learning more about *Miracle Monocle*, or writers who might be interested in joining the ranks of our contributors, we invite you to visit us online: Louisville.edu/miraclemonocle

www.ingramcontent.com/pod-product-compliance
Lightning Source LLC
LaVergne TN
LVHW050948080826
845145LV00004B/1453

* 9 7 8 1 7 3 4 1 2 3 3 2 6 *